BOA CONSTRICTORS

JOHN BANKSTON

ALL ABOUT SNAKES

Creating Young Nonfiction Readers

EZ Readers lets children delve into nonfiction at beginning reading levels. Young readers are introduced to new concepts, facts, ideas, and vocabulary.

Tips for Reading Nonfiction with Beginning Readers

Talk about Nonfiction
Begin by explaining that nonfiction books give us information that is true. The book will be organized around a specific topic or idea, and we may learn new facts through reading.

Look at the Parts
Most nonfiction books have helpful features. Our *EZ Readers* include a Contents page, an index, a picture glossary, and color photographs. Share the purpose of these features with your reader.

Contents
Located at the front of a book, the Contents displays a list of the big ideas within the book and where to find them.

Index
An index is an alphabetical list of topics and the page numbers where they are found.

Picture Glossary
Located at the back of the book, a picture glossary contains key words/phrases that are related to the topic.

Photos/Charts
A lot of information can be found by "reading" the charts and photos found within nonfiction text. Help your reader learn more about the different ways information can be displayed.

With a little help and guidance about reading nonfiction, you can feel good about introducing a young reader to the world of *EZ Readers* nonfiction books.

Mitchell Lane
PUBLISHERS

2001 SW 31st Avenue
Hallandale, FL 33009
www.mitchelllane.com

First Edition, 2019.

Author: John Bankston
Designer: Ed Morgan
Editor: Sharon F. Doorasamy

Names/credits:
Title: Boa Constrictors / by John Bankston
Description: Hallandale, FL : Mitchell Lane Publishers, [2019]

Series: All About Snakes

Library bound ISBN: 9781680203073

eBook ISBN: 9781680203080

EZ readers is an imprint of Mitchell Lane Publishers

Photo credits: Getty Images, Freepik.com

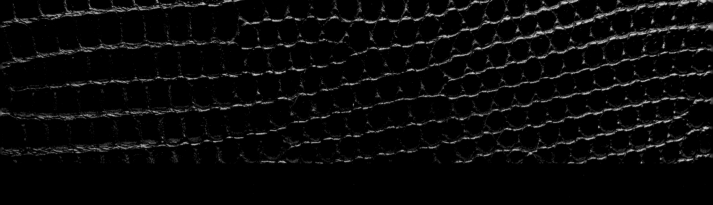

CONTENTS

The boa constrictor waits. Its prey approaches. When it gets close, the boa attacks!

Boa constrictors are nonvenomous snakes famous for squeezing or constricting their prey to death.

Boas are cold-blooded. To keep cool, boas lie inside a hollow log, a burrow, or a cave. They warm up by lying in the sun.

Adult boas are approximately 13 feet (4 meters) long. They can weigh more than 100 pounds (45 kilograms).

Unlike most snakes, boas don't lay eggs. They give birth to 50 or 60 squirming baby boas. Baby boas are two feet long.

Boa constrictors live in South American countries such as Brazil and French Guiana. This is their natural habitat.

In lush rain forests, boas are often green. In areas with clay or mud, boas can be red or brown. There are also yellow boas and ones with different patterns.

Boas are hunted for their skin. They are captured as pets. In some places they are endangered.

19

The best place to see a boa constrictor is at your local zoo.

INTERESTING FACTS

- In the United States, more than 13 million reptiles are kept as pets, according to the Department of Agriculture. This includes boa constrictors. Most are kept for less than one year.

- Boas eat bats. In South America, some people keep boa constrictors to keep bats away.

- The longest boa constrictor ever discovered was 18 feet long.

- The boa constrictor has no eyelids.

- When boas get upset, they hiss. A boa constrictor's hiss can be heard 100 feet away.

PARTS OF A BOA CONSTRICTOR

Head
The snake has one eye on each side of its head. The lower jaw is loosely attached to the upper jaw. This lets it open wide. Its sense of smell is in its mouth. The tongue helps bring in odors.

Teeth
The mouth is lined with small, hooked teeth that are used for grabbing and holding prey. It does not use its teeth to chew. It swallows its prey whole.

Body
Snakes have a backbone made up of many vertebrae attached to ribs. The boa has more than 200 vertebrae. People have 33. The snake's vertebrae expand when it eats. Boas also have hind leg bones. Boas may be related to lizards who had legs.

Tail
The thinner part of the snake where there are no ribs.

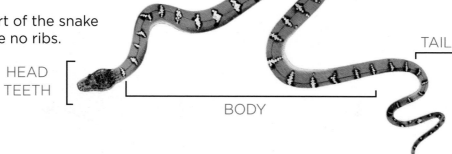

HEAD
TEETH

BODY

TAIL

GLOSSARY

burrow
A hole in the ground made by an animal to live in or hide

constricting
Coiling tightly around prey

endangered
At risk of dying out completely unless protected

habitat
The area where animals live

nonvenomous
Not poisonous

prey
An animal that is hunted by another animal

FURTHER READING

Books

Hoena, Blake, and Brady Barr. *Everything Reptiles: Snap Up All the Photos, Facts, and Fun.* Washington, DC: National Geographic Society, 2016.

Kenan,Tessa. *It's a Boa Constrictor!* Minneapolis, MN: Lerner Classroom, 2017.

Lanser, Amanda. *Boa Constrictor*. Minneapolis, MN: Abdo Publishing Company, 2014.

Spilsbury, Louise. *Boa Constrictor. Killer King of the Jungle*. New York: Windmill Books, 2014.

On the Internet

http://animals.sandiegozoo.org/animals/boa

https://www.nationalgeographic.com/animals/reptiles/b/boa-constrictor/

WORKS CONSULTED

Baker, Christopher P. *National Geographic Traveler: Costa Rica*. Washington, DC: National Geographic Society, 2013.

Ariosto, David. "NYPD uncovers stash of exotic animals." *CNN Wire*, September 8, 2012.

Brumfield, Ben. "What's that? Boa constrictor slinks out of San Diego toilet." *CNN Wire*, January 8, 2015.

Ornes, Stephen. "Giant snakes invading North America." *Science News for Kids*, October 28, 2009.

Milius, Susan. "Boa suffocation is merely myth." *Science News*, August 22, 2015.

University of Florida. "At 2,500 Pounds And 43 Feet, Prehistoric Snake Is Largest On Record." *ScienceDaily*, February 4, 2009. Available online. https://www.sciencedaily.com/releases/2009/02/090204112217.htm.

INDEX